Master the Maze

Kate Scott

Contents

OXFORD
UNIVERSITY PRESS

You are here

Hello, I'm Mini Marvel. My dad Macro Marvel and I invented Micro World. This is one of the books that inspired **Maze Craze**.

Did you know?

This book has challenges for you to complete. The caption gives you an instruction to follow so you can complete the challenge.

Starting at one of the arrows, try to reach the castle.

 # Think and remember

What do you think it would be like to get lost in a maze? Can you remember what happened when Team X and Mini were in the hedge maze in Micro World?

Mini's Top Spot

Can you find these instructions in the book?

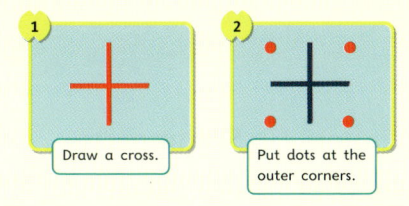

1. Draw a cross.
2. Put dots at the outer corners.

Can you guess what you will have created by the end of step 6?

Before you read

Suffix spotter

- Read the words.

  fanci**ful**   merci**less**   dizzi**ness**   easi**ly**

- The letters in **bold** are suffixes.

- The root words have more than one syllable and end in 'y', e.g. fancy, mercy, dizzy, easy.

- Change the final 'y' to an 'i' before you add one of the suffixes -ful, -less, -ness, -ly.

What does it mean?

maize – a tall plant that produces cobs of corn

permanent – lasting for a very long time, not temporary

Time to find out ...

As you read, use the Expert Tip **Summarize the text** to help you answer this question:

- *Are all mazes made for people to get lost in?*

Walk this maze!

Picture yourself in a maze like this. The hedges are much taller than you, so you can't see where to go. You turn right, then left, then right again and come to a **dead end**. You want to go back the way you came but you can't remember the way.

It feels as if the number of paths is limitless. Will you ever find your way to the middle?

What is a maze?

A maze is a set of paths with twists and turns. In some drawn or written mazes, you solve a puzzle to find a way through. In real-life mazes, if you choose the correct paths you will get to the middle or the other side. Often there is something interesting to see when you get there.

Could you find your way to the middle of this maze?

There is a turret in the middle of this one!

Mazes come in all kinds of shapes and patterns. In some mazes, the design is quite simple. Other mazes are extremely complicated.

This maze has bridges, so the paths go under and over each other. This is sometimes called a 'weave maze'.

Explore the types of maze

Mazes with one path

This type of maze has a single twisting path that takes you to the middle. You have to go all the way around the paths – it might cause dizziness!

Mazes with only one path are often called 'labyrinths' (*say* lab-uh-rinths).

one very long path

start

Mazes with *lots* of paths

Other types of mazes have lots of paths and **junctions**. It's unclear which paths go to the middle, and some of the paths go nowhere or in circles. After a few hopeless dead ends, you might wish you were in a labyrinth!

How would it feel to wander around this maze, with the hedges towering above you?

start   junction   dead end

Mazes with rules

This is a 'number maze'. You have to do sums to find the right **route** to the other side!

Can you show Rex the way to Mini? Start on the 1, and add 6 each time to work out which number he should step on next. Trace the route with your finger.

54	40	36	21	11	7	1	←
42	44	29	17	19	13	5	35	59	66
48	38	33	31	25	27	34	15	77	81
51	46	41	37	23	84	86	102	99	93
70	52	49	43	45	91	97	103	108	112
53	50	55	56	64	85	88	109	116	90
60	76	61	67	73	79	96	115	119	98
80	72	68	78	82	94	118	121	→	

'Logic mazes' have rules which you must follow to find your way through. The word 'logic' means working out a problem step by step.

Start at the stripy star. You can only step on to a shape with the same pattern **or** shape. Trace the route to the spotted square.

end

Mazes that are built or grown

Number mazes and logic mazes are puzzles drawn on paper or on computers, but most mazes are for people to actually walk around in. The most common type is a hedge maze, made out of bushes that are grown and clipped into shape, but mazes can be made from all kinds of materials.

This maze is made of stone.

maize (also known as corn)

This maze is made of maize! It was created by cutting paths into a field of plants.

A mirror maze like this might cause dizziness!

This maze is made of wooden logs.

Could you read your way to the centre of this book maze?

Ancient mazes

Mazes have been created by humans for thousands of years. Over 2400 years ago, a **historian** called Herodotus described a maze he had seen in Egypt. He said it was more impressive than the Egyptian pyramids, but unluckily the maze has not survived.

This grass labyrinth is in England. It is unclear who made it but it is many hundreds of years old.

Mosaics are pictures made from very small tiles. This **Roman** mosaic is a labyrinth that you can walk around on. It is about 1700 years old.

This **Ancient Greek** coin is about 2400 years old. It has a labyrinth on the back.

The minotaur

A story about a maze has also survived since Ancient Greek times.

In the legend, King Minos kept a monster called the 'minotaur' in the middle of a maze. This maze was known as a labyrinth, even though it had lots of paths.

This ancient mosaic shows the minotaur.

The minotaur was part bull and part human. It was put in the maze so it could not get out and eat everyone, but sometimes the **merciless** king sent people in to become its dinner ...

A prince called Theseus (*say* Thee-see-us) came to battle the minotaur and undo the wickedness of the king. A clever princess called Ariadne (*say* Aree-add-nee) gave him a ball of string and told him to unwind it as he walked through the maze.

Bravely, Theseus entered the maze. He defeated the minotaur and then followed his string trail out to safety.

Without Ariadne's string, Theseus would have been trapped forever.

Theseus battles the minotaur

A-mazing mazes

Some mazes also make pictures! Maze **designers** can cleverly arrange the paths so that they form shapes when seen from above.

Which animals can you see?

This **fanciful** maze makes the shape of a dinosaur!

This maze won a world record for being the biggest permanent maze. It covers over 35 square kilometres! From the air, its hedges make the shape of a massive elk.

Did you know?

Permanent mazes last for years. Temporary mazes, like this ice maze, last for a much shorter time.

Record-breaking mazes

These wonderful mazes have also won world records.

This is the oldest surviving hedge maze. It was planted in about 1690.

This maze won the record for being the largest **vertical** maze in the world. It would be very difficult to walk along its paths!

Groundbreaking mazes

Some mazes help us to learn new things. In 1882, a scientist called John Lubbock built the first maze for insects. He wanted to learn how easily ants could find their way when the maze changed.

Scientists often use mazes to test how animals think. In 1901 another scientist, William Small, made the first maze for rats. He wanted to see if they could remember the way through a complicated set of paths.

This rat should go around its maze. It's cheating!

Maze patterns

The junctions and twisting paths of mazes can be used to make interesting patterns. These patterns are not real mazes but they look playful and fun.

Try drawing your own maze-style pattern.

Maze-like patterns are not just made by people. They can be seen in nature too!

The shape of this coral looks like a maze.

Our fingertips have little maze patterns on them!

This cabbage has a maze pattern inside.

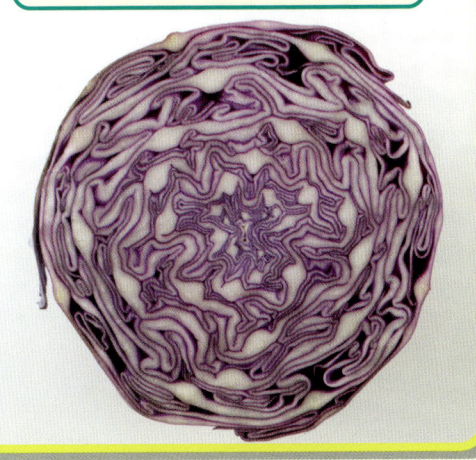

The **veins** on this leaf look like a maze.

Solve a maze!

Mazes can be helpful for scientists, or make beautiful patterns, but they are mainly for fun. Try getting lost in a maze right now ...

Have a go at this maze! Start at the arrow – can you reach the middle?

Starting at one of the arrows, try to reach the castle.

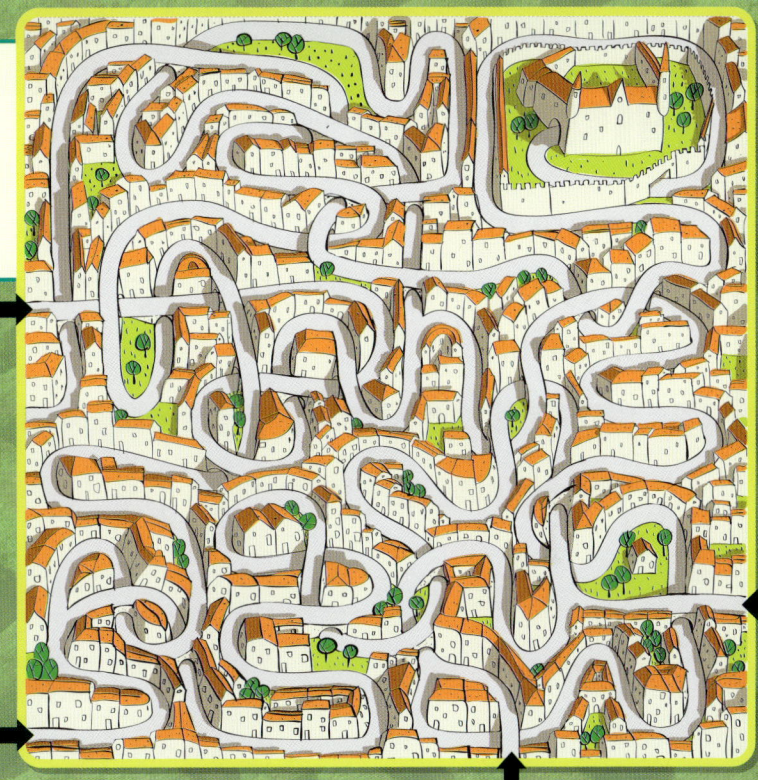

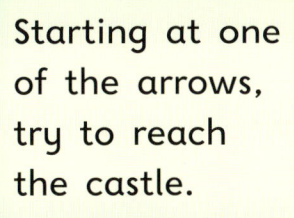

2 x 8 = ?

What is 2 x 8? The arrow that shows the answer is the path to the gold.

16

80

28

32

Make a maze!

There are lots of ways to make a maze. First, try drawing a labyrinth – a maze with just one path.

1 Draw a cross.

2 Put dots at the outer corners.

3 Join up these two points.

4 Join up the next two points.

5

Join up the next two points again.

6

Draw the last line.

You've drawn a labyrinth! Think about what might be in the middle: a nice surprise, or a monster like the minotaur?

Now you can draw a maze that has lots of paths.

1

Draw the centre of the maze.

2

Draw a path to the centre, with lots of turns and corners.

3

Add lots of paths branching off from the first path. Remember to put in some dead ends and junctions. You've drawn a maze!

Build a maze

You can also make a maze from things like:

- cardboard boxes
- pens and pencils
- pasta
- pebbles or stones
- shells
- beads.

This maze is made from cardboard strips.

In some computer games you can build a maze from blocks, lines or dots.

Mazes help us master many skills. They teach us how to solve problems and how to remember directions. They help us practise maths and logical thinking in order to unlock the answers to problems and puzzles.

Most of all, they let us explore and have fun!

Which was your favourite maze?

Glossary

Ancient Greek   made by people from Greece between about 800 BC and 30 BC

dead end   a path or road that has one end blocked off

designer   someone who plans how something will be built or made

fanciful   something that comes from the imagination

historian   someone who studies the past

junction   a place where you have to choose between different paths

merciless   harsh and heartless

Roman   made by people from the Roman Empire between the 8th century BC and the 5th century AD

route   the way you go to get to a place

vein   a tiny tube that carries liquids like blood or sap

vertical   something that is upright

Index

Now you have read ...

Master the Maze

 **Stop and check it makes sense – take action**

Which one of these mazes is *permanent* and which one
is *temporary*?

ice maze

stone maze

 **Summarize the text**

Are all mazes made for people to get lost in? Look at these
mazes and think about what they are made for.